Conferences for Smarties

A practical guide to
maximizing the benefits of
attending conferences

Marna Hayden

Copyright © 2005 Marna Hayden. All rights reserved. This book, or parts thereof, may not be reproduced or transmitted in any form without the express written permission of the author; exceptions are made for brief excerpts used in published reviews.

Published by Hayden Resources Inc.

ISBN: 0-9741428-1-6

Printed in the U.S.A.

This publication contains information from many sources and gathered from personal experience. It is published for general reference and not intended to be a substitute for independent verification by readers when necessary and appropriate. The book is sold with the understanding that neither the author nor the publisher is engaged in rendering any legal, accounting, or other professional advice. The author and publisher disclaim any personal liability, directly or indirectly, for advice or information presented within.

Cover design: Peter Wohlsen, Wohlsen Design, LLC
Editing & interior design: Karl Barndt, Electric Ink, Ltd.

This book is available at quantity discounts upon request. For more information contact:

Hayden Resources Inc.
3456 Park Place
Bethlehem, PA 18017
610 866-6607
marna.hayden@haydenhr.com

DEDICATION

This book is dedicated to all CEOs and leaders who believe in lifelong learning and support their valued staff by providing opportunities for continuous education, and to all my wise and kind friends from the Society for Human Resource Management.

Contents

Acknowledgements .... *vii*
Introduction .... *ix*

CHAPTER 1
The Selection and Approval Process 1

Selecting the Best Conference 1
Expense Justification...3
Request for Attendance...5
Location 6
Transportation 6
Vacation 7
Hotels..8
Pre- or Post-conference Workshops 10

CHAPTER 2
Preparing for the Conference 11

Conference Checklist...11
Checklist..18
Conference Goal Plan..18

CHAPTER 3
Attending the Conference 19

Arriving at the Airport and Hotel 19
Early On-site Registration 20
First-time Conference Attendee...............................20
Shuttles..21
Business Cards 21
Selecting Sessions..22
Speakers..25

v

Exhibitors and Vendors 27
Giveaways and Stuff 29
Prize Drawings 30
Social Events 31
Networking 32
Communication during the Conference 37
Conference CDs 37
Conference Materials 38
Message Center 39
Meeting Places 39
Bookstore 40
Wake-up Calls 40
Expense Tracking 40
Badges, Buttons, and Bows 40
The Conference Host 41

CHAPTER 4
Highlights of the Conference   43

Highlights of Conference Attendance 43

CHAPTER 5
After the Conference   47

Take a Break 47
Reporting on the Conference 47
Organize Information for Easy Access 49

CHAPTER 6
Conclusions and Smarties' Top Ten Tips   51

Smarties' Top Ten Tips 52

Appendix A 55
Appendix B 57
Appendix C 59
Appendix D 61

Acknowledgements

I would like to thank and recognize the following contributors for sharing their ideas and suggestions for this book: Ed Anderson, Mary Cheddie, Judy Clark, Bette Francis, Cornelia Gamlem, Cindy Hornaman, Alicia Horbaczewski, Wanda Lee, Thomas Mobley, Carol Morgan, David Oleksa, Beth Orenstein, Janet Parker, Susan Post, Libby Sartain, Dorothy Stubblebine, Martin Walsh, and Ed White

VIII CONFERENCES FOR SMARTIES

Introduction

Most competitive companies today reserve dollars for their key professionals and managers' continuing education and attendance at professional conferences. This practice benefits the company and also provides a good retention tool for employees.

Despite the cost of these benefits, often neither the company nor the employee attending takes full advantage of the opportunities presented by conferences. Management does not ask for an accounting of the conference and employees do not report what they have learned or how attending the conference will result in positive changes.

I have written this book to offer conference attendees some strategies for maximizing their experience. Within these pages I also offer a means for management to understand and measure the value and benefits of the conference for the company.

My career as a human resources professional has taught me to look for win-win situations between employees and management and to help both parties come to a meeting of the minds. Although I write these tips mostly for the attendees, their employers will also greatly benefit whenever a conference attendee can maximize his or her conference experience.

x Conferences for Smarties

CHAPTER 1

The Selection and Approval Process

Selecting the Best Conference

Time and money limit us from attending every conference in our field. To select the best ones, look for conferences that will help you perform your job to the best of your ability now and in the future. Conference attendance is a major factor in an individual's strategic plan for career and professional development.

Marty Walsh of the SHRM Foundation states three major reasons for attending a conference:

1. Develop professionally by improving your knowledge and skills;

2. Increase your business and professional network;

3. Do business, such as scouting out new products/ideas in the exhibit hall.

Before you decide which conference to attend, make sure conference expenses are included in your company's annual budget.

Research conferences through your company, the Internet, fellow professionals and the professional associations for your field. When in doubt, start with the major conference in your profession. This conference will most likely have the broadest choice of sessions and offer up-to-date coverage of general trends and hot topics.

When I was a senior manager, I alternated every other year between attending the largest conference in my industry and the largest conference in my field. I thought this strategy worked well for me until I realized that I got far more out of the conference in my field and was still able to meet people from my industry there. You will have to discover what works for you. Find people who have attended conferences in your field and ask them for recommendations.

When I asked a number of attendees how they chose conferences, the most common answers were: programs and sessions offered, speakers, time and length of conference, cost, location, and relevance to area of responsibility. The reputation of the organization offering the conference also figured into their decision.

Libby Sartain, Senior Vice President/Human Resources for Yahoo, states: "I find that professional associations do a better job than for-profit conferences because they share a commitment to my profession."

Tom Mobley, partner of Tomcat HR Consulting, selects his national conference for two reasons: the conference is always excellent and he has a "core group of people" with whom he attends. That conference provides him with up-to-date information and the opportunity to network with other professionals.

Exhibitors select their conferences with a great deal of care. Their decisions are based on hard numbers and a cost/benefit analysis of their return on investment.

Ed White, Regional Account Manager for Orasure Technologies, says: "I look at the target audience, the potential number of attendees, the conference agenda, and past history of the event." He then evaluates that information to determine if that conference is a good use of his conference budget. As a vendor, he also tracks the number of leads against the cost of the conference and the sales gained as a result. Comparing the profits generated to the cost of the conference determines success or failure.

Expense Justification

If you are the senior manager in your department, attending a major conference may be a given. If not, you may have to do a little selling.

To justify the expense, go back to your company's strategic plan and your department's role in it. Think about what you need to learn to achieve these goals and how that knowledge will affect your future contribution to the company. In other words, determine the deliverables.

If you base your request on what you will gain from the conference that relates directly to strategic initiatives, you will have a better chance of winning approval. Another selling point: relate past achievements to information you attained from attending a previous conference. Be sure and let your managers know they are getting a return on their investment.

Before leaving for a conference, always ask your supervisor if there are any special sessions you should attend and, if yes, be sure to bring him/her back information on that topic.

Professional associations usually give a conference discount for members. If you don't belong to an association, sometimes joining at conference time can provide a savings. In the event that your company does not reimburse your membership fee, consider paying it out-of-pocket and taking the expense as a tax deduction. If you are serious about your profession, the value of membership in a professional association will far exceed the personal expense. The information you can obtain will enhance your professional knowledge and be well worth the annual fee.

Bette Francis, Director, Human Resources & Administration for Strategic Products & Services, states: "If your company is paying for you to attend, or you plan to request reimbursement, link content to organizational issues. Be ready to invest in your own development. If you are not willing to pay for the conference yourself, it's probably not a compelling conference for you or your company."

Fortunately, most companies pay for their employees' development. However, there are times when a conference was not included in my employer's budget or was deemed necessary for my job at the time. If I felt strongly about attending that conference, I would use my own money and vacation time to attend. I saw that expense as an investment in my future. I would not recommend doing this if it causes a problem with management. Today, as a consultant, I continue to attend the same national conference for which my employer once paid.

Request for Attendance

Once you have selected a conference, make a formal request to attend to management. Be sure to follow your company's approval process. If your company does not have one, I have attached a sample request form you can use (Appendix A.)

If you can show how your attendance will benefit the company, you most likely will get approval. Review your company's current goals and priorities, your department's needs, and your own personal interests so that all will be satisfied by the conference.

When you return, make a report to management, and always thank your company for sending you. I have attached a sample form for reporting on a conference if your company does not have one (Appendix B.)

Location

Location can be tricky. Some associations, for example, will not schedule a conference in a popular vacation destination, like Hawaii. They fear that managers will not approve attendance because attendees might be tempted to enjoy the islands and not attend sessions. Airfare and hotel may also be more expensive. Other conference organizers purposely select attractive locations to lure attendees. If the conference truly focuses on learning, then location will be of less concern. Distance does not always mean higher cost; sometimes flights to a major city or resort area are cheaper than those held in closer locations or not near major hubs.

Transportation

Plan early, but do not necessarily book your flight too far in advance. Listen to advice of the travel agent or airlines and check out fares on the Internet. When a fare seems reasonable, book your flight. Don't wait too long; flights to popular destinations can fill fast. Don't put yourself or your company in the position of either paying too much or not being able to get to your destination at your desired date and time.

Airline fares are often cheaper when you stay over Saturday night. Consider staying if the cost of the extra night at the hotel doesn't increase the total bill. That extra day can give you a little more time to relax, plan and organize.

Take advantage of frequent flyer programs and, whenever possible, use the same carrier, providing rates are comparable. Most companies let employees keep their frequent flyer miles, which is a nice bonus. When I was traveling frequently, my airline would bump me up to first class at no extra charge for almost every flight. It made traveling a pleasure. These better seats are sometimes blocked out for such "elite" flyers. As you gain experience with air travel, you'll become very familiar with connecting airports and their procedures. However, if your company makes all of the travel arrangements, let it.

If the destination is close and you plan to drive, consider carpooling. It saves money and the companionship can be more enjoyable than traveling alone. Just be certain everyone shares the same schedule and take into account not only mileage (gas), but also tolls and parking when splitting costs.

Vacation

Combining a conference with vacation can sometimes be a great idea. Because conference locations often require travel and may be located at popular vacation destinations, you might wish to add a few vacation days to the trip, either before or after the conference. Such scheduling can save you money on transportation, and your family can look forward to your annual conference and new experiences. Many major conferences have spouse and/or family activities for a reasonable, additional cost if they wish to accompany you to the conference. In some cases, babysitting arrangements are offered. You may wish to explore some of these options.

However, if you bring family members with you, don't forget why you are attending the conference. It's not just the sessions. Don't neglect your networking time with other professionals. It's important, because much of your learning experience at a conference is informal. Most professional people enjoy "talking shop," which can be very boring to your family. To avoid these conflicts, keep your conference and family activities separate. This way, your combination conference/vacation will be as stress free and spontaneous as possible. You'll gain the information you came for *and* have fun with your family.

Hotels

If you book early, you can get a wider choice of accommodations, ranging from the more expensive "conference headquarters" hotel to the local Holiday Inn or Hampton Inn.

Remember to take advantage of frequent stay incentive programs offered by hotel chains if you are enrolled in their program. When you book your stay, give the front desk your member number or assign the points earned for your stay to your airlines' frequent flyer program. For years, I wasted those benefits by not bothering to enroll. If you don't have a card, ask the hotel if it has a program, and join. Those points can add up to free stays and specials.

To be closest to most activities and networking, I suggest booking immediately with the conference's main hotel, using your own credit card if you have not yet received formal approval to attend the conference. You can always cancel the reservation without penalty (within the guidelines given by the hotel) if it turns out you won't need the reservation. After you receive approval, your company can reimburse you for the charges to your credit card or you can bill the charges to a company card.

If cost is an issue, find a roommate and share the room expenses. If you do not have a friend from home, consider asking a professional associate you have met before at a conference. It's a great way to exchange professional information and get to know that person better. I have friends who always room with "conference friends" from other parts of the country. It's a great time to catch up.

At my last conference, I roomed with a colleague from another part of the country. I always look forward to seeing her at the annual conference and by rooming together we had a great time visiting and sharing ideas. We plan to do it again this year.

If you are hesitant to share a room, keep in mind that you probably won't spend much time in your room, except to sleep. If you are a light sleeper, bring earplugs and a sleep mask.

Pre- or Post-conference Workshops

If the conference offers pre-conference or post-conference sessions that look beneficial, schedule those as well and plan accordingly.

Often these workshops have excellent national presenters, fewer attendees, and more in-depth coverage of the topics. They are also good places to make new contacts.

CHAPTER 2

Preparing for the Conference

Conference Checklist

Sometimes, getting away from the office can be a major challenge. Keep a checklist and follow these tips to make your life easier:

1. Book your hotel early. Check the location, including the proximity to the conference center, the shuttle schedule, and where the various social activities are scheduled. You don't want to be on the outskirts of the city and have to worry about transportation.

2. Check travel arrangements early, ask for all discount rates, and use the same airline carrier, if possible, to amass frequent flyer miles or get free upgrades. Be sure to specify the seat you want on the plane. Most airlines let

you go online to select your seats in advance. However, they will not assign exit row seats until you are at the airport. If you need the extra leg room, it's worth arriving early.

3. As soon as you get approval, book the conference. Many conferences offer early bird registration discounts. Take advantage of them.

4. Look through the advance program and select the sessions you wish to attend. If the featured speaker has written a book and you want it, buy a copy and bring it along. Reading the book in advance can make the speech or session more meaningful. Check to see if there is an opportunity to get it signed. Though you can usually buy speakers' books at the conference bookstore, the lines can be long. At a recent conference, Queen Noor was a keynote speaker and her book, *Leap of Faith: Memoirs of an Unexpected Life,* was sold at the conference bookstore. She remained after her speech to sign copies of her book, but the lines were very long. Those attendees who already had her book moved to the front of the line for the signing. I can't help but think that those people who had read her book beforehand must have found her speech even more powerful.

5. To get the most out of sessions, write a list of specific questions you want answered and attach it to the applicable session. If the

description about what is covered in the session is unclear, call the 800 number of the conference and ask the program department for clarification.

6. Review the vendor list and highlight the vendors you wish to see.

7. Before the conference you will receive advertising and invitations from vendors in the mail. Many of these pieces provide the vendor's booth number and demonstration schedule or invite you to enter a drawing or attend a reception. Prioritize these and save them in numerical order by booth number. That way, when you visit the exhibition hall at the conference, you can see these vendors in order, saving valuable time.

8. You may want to review a map of the exhibition hall to see how it is laid out and where key vendors are located.

9. Some vendors' cards may request information from you. Fill them out in advance to save time later.

10. Reserve time to see special demonstrations. If vendors are having drawings for giveaways, be sure to stop by to swipe your scanner card or drop off a business card. Prioritize these stops as well.

11. Sometimes the exhibit hall has a food and drink reception. Generally, I make vendor

visits a priority and eat and drink later after the exhibit hall is closed.

12. RSVP to the invitations you want to attend and fill in these extra activities on your daily conference schedule.

13. If you intend to add some vacation time to the conference, get prior approval for the time off. This can be a cost-effective way to see more of the country. Consider having your family join you for the conference if there are good spouse/children programs or have them join you before or after the conference.

14. If you want to reroute your trip home for vacation or side trips, reimburse your company for the difference in the return trip. It still could save you money.

15. If you plan to spend time outside the conference, pick up a travel book about the area in advance. The information provided by your hotel and conference welcome booth may not be sufficient. If you are a member of AAA or another travel club, use its services to order travel information or make trip reservations. You also can find extensive information by searching the Internet.

16. Packing and taking the right clothes is important. You want to travel as light as you can, but have the appropriate items for all occasions. Here are some of my guidelines:

- Check the conference materials to see what the dress code is. Most are "business-casual" with one night that is more formal. Business casual does not mean jeans, T-shirts, tank tops, sneakers, etc. Remember, you are representing your company as well as yourself, so dress comfortably, but professionally. It is better to err on the side of being too formal than not formal enough, since the former shows respect and professionalism.

- Pack comfortable shoes; you will do a lot of walking and standing. Mary Cheddie, VP/HR for Orvis, says, "Wear the most comfortable shoes possible; it's not about fashion; it's about staying upright and being pain free."

- Even if you're in New Orleans during the summer, take a jacket or sweater. Conferences are held indoors, where air conditioning may be too cold for your comfort. You may wish to wear your jacket or heaviest clothing on the plane.

- Use wheeled bags and lightweight luggage. Pack suits, jackets, dresses, shirts or blouses on hangers and cover them with clear plastic from the cleaners. You do not want to spend time ironing or money on room service. Use travel-friendly fabrics when you can, such as silk, microfiber, and knits. If you cannot pack items on wire hangers, select fabrics that roll well. Other items can be wrapped in plastic if they wrinkle easily.

- Bring mix and match clothing with a basic color theme for shoes, belts, handbags, etc.

- Bring medications and a change of clothing in your carry-on. Avoid packing certain items (tweezers, scissors, and jackknives) that airlines no longer permit in carry-ons. Check ahead with the airline about cameras and film. I still use a leaded bag to protect my film and always take extra batteries. Generally, I have my film and camera in my carry-on, but place batteries in my checked luggage. I have run across this rule on some airlines.

- Make a list of all suitcase contents and keep it separate from your baggage. If you have a passport, make a copy and place one in each of your bags. If not, at least have a business card or your name and address inside each bag.

- Bring *lots* of business cards. Although most conferences use scanner cards for exhibitors, you will still want to exchange cards with new friends and contacts.

- If you bring a cell phone, BlackBerry or laptop, be sure to bring the charger. If you bring a laptop, don't lose it. (Airlines say more laptops are left at security than any other item!)

- Select good reading material for the plane and place it in your carry-on bag. If you haven't had time to read the conference materials and select sessions and vendors to see, this is a good time to do it.

- Remember to bring your credit and ATM cards and take enough cash with you, including singles for tipping.

17. Make all last-minute arrangements at home and in the office:

- Set your email and telephone voicemail to let correspondents know when you are not available (both office and home).

- Delegate, or teach, someone to sort your mail, handle what can be handled, and prioritize the rest for you when you return.

- Leave emergency numbers where you can be reached.

- Wrap up as many projects as you can before you leave.

- Notify the Post Office if you wish to have your mail held while you are away.

- Take care of pets, plants, and family arrangements, as needed.

- Confirm your flight.

- Arrive at the airport early, with your ticket or e-ticket and a photo ID.

Checklist

A quick checklist may be found in Appendix C. Customize it to meet your needs.

Conference Goal Plan

Before attending the conference, Marty Walsh of SHRM suggests doing the following: "Make a quantitative worksheet with your goals, such as make 5 new contacts, visit X vendors in the following areas, etc.," along with the sessions you selected.

CHAPTER 3

Attending the Conference

Arriving at the Airport and Hotel

If possible, research ground transportation between the airport and your hotel before you leave home. Your pre-registration packet probably contains information and perhaps a discount coupon for a shuttle service. If you're lucky, the hotel will have a free shuttle; but you may need to call for it.

If I must buy my shuttle ticket, I do so as soon as I have disembarked from the plane. It's a good time to do it because the lines are often shorter and you must wait for baggage anyway. Shuttle roundtrips provide a discount, but often you need to call a day ahead to schedule your return trip. You also might not need that return shuttle trip. It may be more convenient, and even cheaper, to share a cab with someone you meet at the conference who has a return flight about the same time as you. Quite a few times I have been offered a ride, or have found friends leaving for the airport at the same time, so I usually buy a one-way ticket. This is an individual preference. When you arrive at the hotel, your room may not be ready, so be prepared to check your bags. Often, you can find other conference attendees in the lobby or lounge.

Early On-site Registration

When you reach your hotel and check in, register as early as possible for the conference. If you cannot check into your room and registration is open, you should do it then. Confirm the scheduled hours for registration either from your conference materials, the hotel list of activities on your room TV, or in the lobby. Avoid the lines of last-minute registration. When you pick up your nametag and conference materials, ask if there is special information you should know about the conference.

First-time Conference Attendee

If you are a first-time conference attendee, ask about orientation. If an orientation is offered, it will well be worth your time. If not, ask at the conference information desk about special activities or procedures you should be aware of. For example, there are usually sign-ups for dinner on free nights for people traveling alone. Many long-term friendships have been made this way. Do not spend excessive time with people you normally see at home; this is a time to meet new contacts and get new perspectives.

Alicia Horbaczewski, a graduate of Cornell University, recently attended her first major conference. Her advice is to "take the time before you come to plan out what events/speakers/exhibits you want to visit." Don't waste precious time during the conference doing things that could be planned ahead.

Dorothy Stubblebine, SPHR, Managing Principal, DJS Associates, Inc., advises: "Attach yourself to a conference pro (someone who has done this before) and see how they do it."

Shuttles

If shuttle buses are used, get the schedule and review it. Be at the designated stops early, whether you are riding to the conference center or to a special event. Note the time of the last return trip.

Business Cards

Keep your business cards handy and pass them out. On those cards you receive, make a note on the back to help you remember the contact and jog your memory. Meeting so many people and getting so much information in such a short period of time can be confusing, so have a system.

One of the best investments I made recently is a business card scanner. It cost about $200, but it is worth every penny. Now when I attend a conference or mixer, I run the new business cards through the scanner, and the information comes up on an electronic Rolodex. That information is not only downloaded to my computer, but it's also added to my email address file. You may need to make a few minor corrections, but most information is captured accurately. There is also space in the contact records to add notes.

Selecting Sessions

When selecting sessions, you can't go wrong with the general sessions and keynote speakers. They're usually very good and you shouldn't miss them. For concurrent sessions, get to the room early, especially for the ones you are sure you want to attend or know will be the most popular. Sometimes the seating fills up and you cannot even get into the room. Always have a second choice selected in case this happens to you.

The most common reasons attendees select sessions are:

- The topics are most relevant to their current job responsibilities.

- The topics keep them current with trends, changes and legal implications in their field.

- The session has a new speaker or new topic they want to hear.
- The speaker has a good reputation for being interesting and having good content.
- The topic is a "growth topic" or area they would like to know about that does not fall under their current job responsibilities.
- The topic was suggested to them by their company's management as one that covers areas they plan to change and programs they wish to implement.

Always select your sessions prior to the conference from the conference promotional materials. Plan to attend the sessions which have the essential information you need, as well as the ones that sound interesting. Sometimes there is an advance CD sent with registration materials. This will give you the best idea what the session will cover. However, in most cases, the description in the program is sufficient. If more than one speaker covers the topic, you may wish to check out his or her website for more information. Many conference speakers have a website or, if not, an address where they can be reached.

Take notes on key ideas. Most conference materials include a notebook, but bring your own, just in case. Even if you have a handout or outline to accompany the session, you should write down pertinent thoughts triggered by the discussion or presentation.

Some people will use their laptop to summarize what they have learned the end of each day. Others may use a tape recorder and have the notes typed when they get home.

Experienced conference attendees will tell you not to stay in sessions that aren't satisfying. If a session isn't what you expected—too basic or too advanced—move on to another.

Janet Parker, SVP Corporate Employee Relations for AmSouth Bank, says: "If sessions don't meet your expectations, leave and go to another one. Don't waste time by staying in a session that is not of value." Most large conferences have a broad choice of concurrent sessions, and they range from the basic to the strategic.

Carol Morgan, VP, Labor Relations for Silberline Manufacturing Company, Inc. says, "Always have Plan A and Plan B, just in case the session you wanted to attend is full. Have a basic understanding of the location of the meeting rooms and the layout of the Conference Center." Her comments remind me of a nightmare conference I attended that used two hotels in New York City. Of course, all my second choices were in the other hotel. Even within a single venue, some conference halls can be blocks long! This is another good reason to select the right sessions in the first place, whenever possible.

Libby Sartain, SVP/HR for Yahoo summarizes how she selects sessions: "When I was new in my career, I selected topics related to the work I was currently doing. Later, I went to sessions not related to my specialty so I could be more general vs. special in my career. Often I seek out speakers with topics that I would like to share with my team."

Tom Mobley, partner of Tomcat HR Consulting, notes that he select topics that allow him to find new material to add to his own instructional repertoire. I agree with Tom; the fresh ideas you gain are great to update and upgrade any presentations you may be making. Every time I teach or present an overview of a topic, I want the latest information.

If you are interested in getting the most content out of your conference, attend the early bird sessions scheduled in the morning. These are often some of the best sessions and sometimes have smaller groups. giving you more opportunities to interact and ask questions.

Some professional conferences have special sessions by industry, such as finance, health care, technology, etc. You may wish to attend these to gather more specific information about your industry practices and to meet a good networking group.

Speakers

I cannot tell you how much I have enjoyed the keynote speakers at national conferences. These people come from all walks of life and often share great thoughts and incredible experiences. Don't miss them. Their comments are most always inspirational, thought-provoking and galvanizing. People who are at the top of their field have a lot to share and many good lessons to teach.

Most national-level speakers, even for the concurrent sessions, go through a rather intense screening of credentials and are well-respected in their fields. You can be assured that your session leaders are very good. If you have the opportunity to get a business card from the speakers you liked, do so. Usually, their contact information is also on their PowerPoint slides or handout. Some have a newsletter and others offer a website.

One of my colleagues makes a practice of contacting speakers he likes. He lets them know how much he appreciated the session and usually keeps in touch with them. By doing this, he always has a circle of experts to call on as a sounding board and to give him advice when he needs it. As he has grown in his profession, he shares valuable information with them as well. If his company ever needs a specialist, he has a good list of resources.

Mary Cheddie, a frequent conference speaker, described her best conference experience in 2004: "…while (I was) waiting for the general session doors to open, the person sitting to my left said, 'I heard your speak in 2001—you've changed my life for the better!'"

I understand Mary's feelings well. As an instructor, my greatest satisfaction has come from former students telling me how what I taught them has contributed to their success. Most people have a natural desire to share their knowledge, and they appreciate the recognition. Even national speakers are often very open to staying in touch with their constituents.

If you have access to books or articles the speaker has written, read them to learn more about the speaker. You will also be in a better position to fashion questions you wish answered or clarified at the session. Most speakers save time for Q & A (Questions and Answers), but if they do not, you can write or email them.

Exhibitors and Vendors

The first day of the conference typically offers an open reception with food and drink in the exhibition hall. The hall is then open at scheduled times during the conference. Sometimes the exhibition hall closes before the end of the conference, so be sure and visit your selected vendors early. Check the hours so you can plan appropriately.

I put my vendors in numerical order by booth assignment, which generally is available prior to the conference. I prefer to take a wheeled cart with me to hold vendor literature and other materials I'm likely to receive. When you visit a number of vendors, the takeaways can add up quickly to a heavy load. I load up my cart with vendors' materials during the first open session. This gives me a chance to review those materials. On subsequent days, I return to those vendors with whom I wish to exchange further information.

Don't underestimate the value of getting to know vendors. They are on top of the latest and greatest products that make our jobs easier and more effective. Visiting with them is part of the educational experience. If you don't wish to keep and carry all their literature, don't take it. If you want to read it and then discard what you don't need, do so. Keep their business cards so you will have names and companies to contact in case you need their product or service.

Ed White, exhibitor for Orasure, asks attendees to "be honest and sincere about your intentions to purchase an exhibitor's service or product vs. educating yourself on the latest trends. Vendors expect to be told when someone is not interested and expect an interested customer to answer the call/email/visit when they say they are interested."

Ed further advises: "Be forthright, see as many vendors that you feel can answer the needs of your organization, and ask the same questions to everyone. Great up front preparation makes a wonderful long-term, high-value business relationship."

Mary Cheddie, of Orvis, reveals her strategy: "Review the directory and plan which (vendors) I want to speak with. I also walk every aisle, but don't stop at every vendor."

Bette Francis of Strategic Products and Services views vendors as "subject matter experts."

Carol Morgan, of Silberline Manufacturing Co., says: "I identify services that I need or something that I believe I will be interested in the near future and visit (those vendors) first, then I just walk through. I always look to see where exhibitors are geographically located, in case I want to send them an invitation to be an exhibitor at one of our local conferences."

Tom Mobley, of TomCat, advises attendees to "attend as many evening exhibitor receptions as possible." After the exhibit hall closes down, many of the major vendors will have hospitality suites or events. These gatherings allow you to get to know the vendor better, as well as providing another networking opportunity.

Everyone agrees that pertinent information can be gained by visiting vendors, and it is a great opportunity to have so many vendors in the same place for comparisons of services and products. It can be a real-time saver when you are making a buying decision.

Giveaways and Stuff

I will admit I enjoy the freebies as much as anyone else; and I used to bring back enough office supplies and gadgets for my staff to last the entire year. I had a basket on a table outside my office filled with small toys I had collected at conferences. When the children of employees came to visit, they were allowed to choose a toy from the basket.

Some good giveaways have been books, sample software, and discount coupons. There are always one or two hot, new items at a conference, but they generally go very fast. Recently, one vendor gave away long-stemmed roses with customized inspirational or advertising messages on their petals. If you are so inclined, you can usually pick up free toys for the kids, pens and pencils, sticky pads, staplers, note pads, hats, T-shirts, first-aid kits, luggage tags, mugs, letter openers, stress balls, and all kinds of useful and not-so-useful items. When our children are young, most of us collect a teddy bear, truck or some kind of flashing gimmick to delight them. I have to admit that those companies get exposure; the items are all over my office and home.

Susan Post, Regional Director for the Society for Human Resource Management (SHRM), says she knows people who bring an extra empty suitcase just for things they will bring back from the conference. Others just bring a larger bag for their freebies. I prefer to mail them home. This can be done at the conference center, hotel or local Post Office.

Experienced conference attendees tend to bring back only the educational materials and items they can use. They discard excess literature and gimmicky items they don't need. It's your preference.

Prize Drawings

Prize drawings offered by vendors and sponsors are another perk of conferences. Some of the prizes are pretty substantial, so enter these drawings and be present when the winners are drawn. One of my friends still rues the day she did not stay for the drawing and her name was called. The prize, a vacation for two, had to be awarded to the next name drawn. On a lighter note, I once forced a friend, who said she never wins anything, to enter a drawing. Sure enough, she won a Caribbean vacation for two. (I love to remind her of that; unfortunately, she decided to take her sister instead of me.)

I have won a variety of prizes, including a magnum of champagne, a lovely mantle clock, a giant Mickey Mouse, jewelry, books, TV, free seminars, and many other items. Fortunately, vendors will ship most of the big stuff to your home or office.

Friends have reported winning digital cameras, $100 in cash, a brief case, and free books. Sometimes, the grand prize is the next year's conference fee, paid in full.

Social Events

Social events are fun, break up long days, and provide great networking opportunities. Free newspapers covering the conference events are usually available; you will want to pick them up. If you receive invitations, RSVP when requested and do not crash. Sometimes you can go from one reception to another during the same time period, but do not accept invitations for events you cannot attend. Decide to attend the ones most beneficial to you.

Don't overeat or drink too much. Food and drink are often plentiful, but you want to feel good, so pace yourself. (While I'm mentioning not overeating, consider bringing your workout clothes or bathing suit, if you are into fitness, and try the fitness center or pool at the hotel. I admire anyone who continues their exercise routine while away from home—or for that matter, at home! If there is a fun run or walk, sign up. You will feel good doing it, and for the walkers especially, it is another opportunity to network.)

I have received advice from both new attendees and veterans about not doing things you would regret later, like drinking too much and acting bizarre or juvenile. The people you meet at conferences are fellow professionals, people with whom you may want to establish long-term relationships. Remember that you also represent your company. I don't know anyone who thinks being drunk is attractive and funny, except the person who is drunk. You can have fun without casting your inhibitions to the wind.

One last note about free food and drink. If you don't eat a large breakfast, you often can find free coffee and pastries at the conference center, exhibition hall or early bird sessions.

Networking

Networking is very effective and rewarding, whether you plan ahead or casually meet people at the conference. All my advisors believe networking opportunities are most important. With a little effort, you can develop a large network of contacts that can benefit you when you need advice or a sounding board. Many of these people have had similar experiences and can offer helpful advice.

Formal social gatherings present a number of networking opportunities, but often the best networking occurs by chance. I have met very interesting contacts at the airport, on the ride to the hotel, at check-in, in the elevator, while waiting in line, at meals, in restrooms, on the shuttle bus, in sessions, in the lounge and through other friends.

Before the conference, prepare for networking encounters by writing and memorizing a short description of your job and company. Develop a several specific questions or topics you want to learn more about. Be sure to ask those questions. Here a few examples:

- Has anyone had experience installing XYZ software?

- What incentive plans have worked the best in your company?

- Has anyone used a good consulting firm for making a change in a particular area?

Start with a broad open-ended question to include everyone. Some examples:

- What has been the best new practice in your company this year?

- What part of this conference or which sessions are you most looking forward to and why?

- What is your view of the best way to handle a certain change?

Have some good ideas of your own ready to share as well.

Email makes networking easier today. Stay in touch with new colleagues. The extra effort may save you a lot of time or even money when you have a difficult challenge.

From a self-centered perspective, you can gather a network of contacts from companies for which you may wish to work some day. You can gain much insight into the culture and practices of companies from talking with their employees. Some people have actually had job offers or have recruited employees at a conference. Conferences almost always have a job bank of positions in your field. If you have openings, you may wish to post them.

Carol Morgan, of Silberline Manufacturing, shares this story: "At the most recent national conference, I stopped in to post a job on the computer, and when I came back to check responses and résumés, I found none. Just then, an individual came in and sat down to use the computer next to me. In slight desperation, I turned to him and said, 'I don't believe there is one HR person in Indiana looking for a job.' He stated he was from Indiana and, in the small world category, was from a town very close to where I had a job opening. He knew of a plant closing in August with a very good HR person who was going to be out of work. We exchanged business cards, he sent me her name and I contacted her. After a review of her résumé and a telephone interview, it appears that she is the right person to fill the job."

Carol tells of another situation that involved networking, "Two years ago, I was preparing for union contract negotiations. I met someone at the annual conference who had the same international representative, same union, who had completed negotiations a year earlier. We exchanged business cards and, later, union contracts. We still stay in touch with each other."

Carol added that those contacts alone more than paid for the conferences she attended.

Informal sharing of experiences, combined with the sessions, will give you a good idea of best or successful practices. This will save you time and money and make your workplace better, with the beneficial side effect of developing great professional friendships.

One of my colleagues, Dorothy Stubblebine, advises conference attendees to talk to everyone. She met one of her best friends at a conference fifteen years ago and wrote, "Nancy has been there for me during my husband's death; we vacationed together and, of course, we meet at the annual conference every year. But most of all, we have fun."

Tom Mobley suggests that you "invite people you meet to go out with your groups. This extends the networking base." He adds, "The relationships I have developed have helped me both on a professional and personal level."

When asking Ed White if networking has been of value to him as a vendor, he responds: "Absolutely. It is rare to have (this) many of my partners and customers in one place."

When I was in charge of Marketing for my company, I met people working for similar organizations in other parts of the country who were not direct competitors. We exchanged great ideas that I brought back and implemented in my company. We corresponded for years. The same is true with my friends in Human Resources and consulting, and I'm sure applies to all fields. I have made invaluable contacts over the years, and they are a great source of information and support.

Alicia Horbaczewski, a recent college grad who is new to the conference world, has a different perspective about networking. She stresses making good first impressions and treating the conferences "like job interviews." She feels that while she is evaluating others, they are evaluating her. In her opinion, "schmoozing" takes a lot of work and energy; you need to be ready at any moment for whomever you meet.

All fields have their idiosyncrasies and frustrations. For many attendees, it's energizing to meet new people who understand your field and can offer new ideas and solutions. Meeting with kindred spirits can be a great support system!

One last tip a teacher gave me years ago: When you are talking, you aren't learning. Take time to practice your active listening skills.

Communication during the Conference

If you need to be in touch with home or office by computer, you probably can find connections in your hotel room or at the information center. Some companies expect employees to check-in during the conference, but, in most cases, your office should contact you only if an important issue arises.

Set the protocol at your office before you leave. Have your wireless phone with you, but remember to turn it off during the sessions and even while attending social gatherings. Interruptions can be rude and distracting.

Some attendees keep up with email during the conference; others will not interrupt their conference experience. It's an individual or company preference. Rather than postponing them, Mary Cheddie of Orvis likes to go through and handle all phone or email messages daily. She also advises taking a day's vacation after the conference to "process" the new information she has gathered.

Conference CDs

Today's conferences often provide a free CD in the conference materials that includes the overheads from many sessions. Handouts from the sessions, which are given to session attendees, can sometimes be purchased if you were not able to attend a particular session. Although handouts are usually available, take notes to capture what is important to you and your company. Conferences also sell audiotapes of many sessions. They can fill you in on sessions you were unable to attend or wish to share with others. Keep in mind that audiotapes are generally cheaper if you purchase them at the conference.

Conference Materials

If you get a conference bag, put your name on it immediately; they all look alike. Tie a colored bow or tag to it so someone does not inadvertently take it. Go through the conference materials right away and keep what you need, toss what you do not. Meal tickets or show tickets are often in the bag, so be careful what you discard. Put all tickets in a safe place. Some tickets must be exchanged for specific seats; do this early to assure you get the seating you want.

Go through your materials again every night and remove what you no longer need. If you have too much material to take back with you on the plane, pack and mail it. I usually get a box from the hotel to pack heavy items to mail back to work. The conference centers often have packing services and lockers, which you can use if you prefer. I have found it is easier and no more costly to mail packages from my hotel or from a Post Office, if one is nearby. Either way, shipping such materials is a big help; paper is heavy and the package will probably reach your office by the time you do.

Message Center

Learn to use the message center early. Message centers typically operate in the conference center with computers and your scanner card. Check for your messages periodically. You also can send messages to other attendees, which is far easier than expecting to run into them at a large conference or calling different hotels to see where they are registered.

Meeting Places

Some conferences have special meeting areas. See if there is one of interest at your conference and go there. These might include an international networking lounge, a "certified" lounge, a specific industry room, or a student area.

If you are meeting someone during the conference, be specific about where to meet; some lounge or dining areas are huge.

Much of your learning will be informal, through networking and meeting with colleagues. Be open to new experiences; get out of your comfort zone. Ask questions, share information, and have fun.

Bookstore

Don't forget to visit the conference bookstore while there. Most have a large selection of industry specific literature and the conference speakers' books, accompanied by a schedule of book signings. In addition to books and literature, many of these bookstores carry nice gifts related to your profession.

Wake-up Calls

Even if you brought an alarm clock or wake early by habit, use the hotel's wake-up call system. Play it safe, so you don't miss your first session or have to rush.

Expense Tracking

This can be easy or difficult, depending on your approach. Record your business expenses as they occur. Save receipts and keep them together. If your company has a special expense sheet to turn in, take it with you. Fill it out as you go. Don't forget mileage, tolls, parking, transportation (taxi, shuttle bus, airplane, etc.), meals, gratuities, hospitality, conference materials (tapes, books, etc.), shipping expenses, hotel, telephone calls, and any other business-related expenses. I have attached a generic expense form in Appendix D.

Badges, Buttons, and Bows

All conferences have name badges which serve two purposes: a means for entry to conference activities, and identification for people you meet. Wear your badge throughout the conference activities, but don't forget to place the badge in your pocket when going out on the street for dinner.

Many associations have special buttons or pins to designate a local chapter of the association, a special interest group, a volunteer leader, or other distinction. People often exchange these items at the conference, so if you have access to extras from your organization, bring them along. Some vendors have special pins commemorating the conference and the city. Check with the vendors who carry jewelry.

Ribbons for attendees are also popular and can be picked up at the association's booth, often located in the exhibition hall. These ribbons attach to your name badge and carry designations from First Time Attendee to VIP Leader. They are colorful and fun conversation pieces.

You will see long-time conference attendees adorned like five-star generals. They're usually people who know the ropes; so if you have questions, ask them.

The Conference Host

Get to know the host organization for the conference. It is always nice to have friends at headquarters. If you're a member of the host organization, look into membership benefits you may not be using. Consider volunteering to help with activities that may be of interest to you.

42 Conferences for Smarties

Sometimes, if you volunteer at the conference, your registration fee will be discounted or even waived.

CHAPTER 4

Highlights of the Conference

Highlights of Conference Attendance

A poll of experienced conference attendees reveals the following highlights:

1. Networking with other professionals
2. Keeping up with the greatest thought leadership in their field
3. Sharing ideas
4. Hearing the keynote speakers
5. Obtaining practical information from the sessions
6. Learning about the new products at the Expo
7. Checking out the hot items in the bookstore

Every conference experience is different and people attend for different reasons. One should always be open to new experiences, but set your expectations before you attend. Create a key list of deliverables you wish to obtain from the conference. These will differ every year. In addition to listing the main deliverables for your company, you may wish to set some personal goals for yourself, before and after you attend. Self-improvement is always a good tactic for job security. Make a contract with yourself to adopt certain personal initiatives as a result of the conference.

One of my friends decided to learn more about certification by talking with certified colleagues. She also sought their advice on the best study methods to pass the exam. She had many people to ask and provide opinions on what was valuable to them, allowing her to make a good decision. (She did pass her exam!)

Alicia Horbaczewski, our first-time attendee at the Society for Human Resource Management Annual Conference and Exposition, revealed what she enjoyed the most: "For me, the best part of the conference was the International Networking Lounge. It was the best way for me to meet interesting new contacts because it was a resting place outside... all of the chaos going on inside. In this lounge, you could just relax and have a cup of coffee, and muse over whatever comes to mind... with some new friends who also share your passion for international issues in human resources."

Exceptional speakers were the high point for Janet Parker, SVP AmSouth Bank, who has attended years of conferences. In her opinion, the best "speakers understand the audience and provide information related to the specific group, …(they) can relate experiences to the specific theme of the conference. Colin Powell was by far one of the best keynote speakers we have had at the annual conference. While he didn't speak specifically about HR, he did talk about leadership traits. I have used several of his examples in presentations that I have provided to groups."

Carol Morgan states, "In the last two National SHRM Conferences the networking alone and results from that saved the company more than the cost of several conferences."

Speaking for vendors, Ed White says, "The greatest value is to maximize the view of the brand. This is a marketing event vs. a selling event."

Bob Mobley's response is universal: Relationships and knowledge. His highlights include networking with professionals and obtaining up-to-date information.

CHAPTER 5

After the Conference

Take a Break

If you have the luxury of time, take a day off to decompress after a multi-day conference. A good conference leaves you with a lot of information to sort through. That day off is also a good time to write a report to management listing what you will start or do differently as a result of the experience.

Reporting on the Conference

To get a start on your conference reporting, take some notes at the airport or on the plane when returning from the conference. The conference will still be fresh in your mind and time may not be available when you're back in the office, catching up.

In your formal report, give an overview of the conference, what you learned and what you will change as a result. It need not be lengthy, but it should have substance.

Schedule a meeting with your supervisor to go over the highlights. Establish a plan and timetable to implement changes as a result of your experience. I have attached a sample format in Appendix B that you may find useful if your company does not provide one of its own. Do not miss this opportunity.

Share information on key issues with other members of your company's management team and CEO. Report highlights to them and have a challenging discussion about how these issues would affect their areas and the company as a whole. Win their support before initiating any changes.

After a conference, Mary Cheddie makes a top ten list of "what I can do differently and/or implement (no more than ten)."

Janet Parker makes copies of handouts for her group if the information is valuable for them. Otherwise, she gives a verbal overview.

Carol Morgan also gives a verbal overview and shares her conference CD with those interested. She also has bought tapes of sessions and shared them with management.

Libby Sartain requires team members to share written reports at staff meetings or, in some cases, in one-on-one meetings.

Although many attendees use what they have learned, some do not formally share the wealth of knowledge they have gained. Make a resolution to share what you have learned.

Set some professional development goals for yourself and a timetable to achieve them as a result of attending the conference. These could range from reading a recommended book to joining a professional chapter.

As a follow up, Marty Walsh of SHRM recommends a measurement device used by organizations like Gallup and the Center for Creative Leadership. "They ask participants to write a letter to themselves (about) what they are going to do differently as a result of attending the leadership programs—namely, change in behavior and performance initiatives." Put this letter away and open it in six months. Marty explains why, "So often we come back from conference high as a kite of all the changes we are going to make. Within a week or two, all these good intentions are buried under the daily pressure to put out fires." Make yourself accountable.

Organize Information for Easy Access

Create a special file for the information you've gained and the contacts you've made. My file is separated into professional contacts, topics and vendors. Some conferences still provide a list of attendees, but most of the larger ones have discontinued that practice, so file your business cards either in a separate case or on your computer.

I cannot tell you how many good ideas have been generated or problems solved by calling my professional colleagues. Whether it is a simple or complex topic, I may not have all the answers, but I know where to get them. With a wide circle of contacts, you can find a resource for almost everything.

In times where you need a special sounding board about your own career and where it is heading, some of these friends will be your most objective and confidential resources.

Chapter 6

Conclusions and Smarties' Top Ten Tips

Keep in touch with the key people you have met. Make an email list of new colleagues and vendors with notes to jog your memory. Make a log of resources for future use and add contact names.

Develop proposals based on your findings. Even the smallest pieces of information you have learned could have a large impact on your job or company, such as a new law you are not following to the letter, a new idea how to improve customer service, or a new product to increase efficiency.

Staying abreast of changes in your field and learning best practices and trends for the future will make you a more valuable resource for your company and a more marketable asset when seeking promotion or another position.

Continuing education is part of ongoing improvement and is necessary if you intend to compete in your field or industry. The best security for an individual or a company is being well-informed and constantly learning how to be better. Having a network of resources in your field is also critical to success. The many resources provided by these large conferences can be invaluable to both individuals and companies.

Last of all, don't forget to thank your boss for sending you. It's a sizable expense and I'm sure he/she will feel it was money well spent if you express your appreciation and bring back ideas that improve the quality of work you provide to the organization.

Smarties' Top Ten Tips

1. Review materials before the start of the conference. Make a schedule of events for each day and carry it with you.

2. Share business cards with at least ten new people. Keep in touch with them after the conference.

3. Collect information pertinent to your present and/or future job.

4. Attend sessions where you will have the opportunity to gain new information outside of your current area of responsibility.

5. Get to know vendors and the newest products and services in your industry.

6. Plan extra breaks and flexibility in your day. Wear comfortable shoes and do not overindulge in anything but knowledge. Take care of yourself.

7. Write a report about what you have learned at the conference and share it with others.

8. Set up a resource file for fellow professionals, vendors, speakers and content experts.

9. Formulate a specific plan about what you are going to do or change as a result of your new knowledge.

10. Plan ahead so you can enjoy new experiences and friends. Be spontaneous, but create a good impression. And have fun!

By using these tips, you can be a smart conference attendee and fully enjoy and maximize the experience. Best of luck!

If you have tips and wish to share them for a future edition of this book, please forward them to marna.hayden@haydenhr.com for our next edition. Thank you very much.

APPENDIX A

All forms in the Appendices are available as Adobe Acrobat PDF downloads from the author's website: www.haydenhr.com.

REQUEST FOR CONTINUING EDUCATION

Name:_____   Date of Request:_____

Position:_____   Date of Conference:_____

Description of Program:
_____
_____

Reason for Attendance:
_____
_____

How does this relate to your present or future position in the company?
_____

How does this program support corporate goals?
_____

What are the deliverables you plan to bring back to the company?
_____

Cost: (Include registration, travel, lodging, meals, and all other expenses.)
_____

Is it in budget?   Yes___   No___

If not, please explain:
_____
_____

Signature of Employee:_____

Signature of Supervisor: _____

Signature of Division Head:_____

Request approved_____   Requested denied_____

If denied, reason:
_____
_____

APPENDIX B

REPORT ON CONFERENCE

Name:_____   Name of Conference:_____
Position:_____   Date of Conference:_____

Highlights of Conference:
_____
_____
_____
_____
_____

Deliverables from Conference Attendance:
_____
_____
_____
_____
_____

What will you do differently as a result of attending this conference?
_____
_____
_____
_____
_____

Would you recommend this conference to others in the future?

Yes____   No____   Please explain:
_____
_____
_____
_____

Other Comments:
_____
_____
_____
_____
_____

Signature of Employee:_____ Date:_____

Please send a copy of this report to your supervisor, division head, and Human Resources within one week of returning from conference. Thank you.

Appendix C

Checklist

- ☐ Budget the prior year
- ☐ Obtain approval based on deliverables
- ☐ Take advantage of the "early bird special"
- ☐ Find a room-mate if you wish to save additional money
- ☐ Shop airlines/transportation for the best deals
- ☐ Select sessions prior to arrival, plan daily schedule
- ☐ Plan vacation in conjunction with conference
- ☐ Pack sensibly; make packing list
- ☐ Use bags with wheels
- ☐ Bring lots of business cards
- ☐ Select and visit key vendors
- ☐ RSVP to special invitations
- ☐ Make office arrangements for your absence
- ☐ Make home arrangements for your absence
- ☐ Keep expense records
- ☐ Notate new business cards
- ☐ Plan for shipping/transportation of conference materials
- ☐ Complete report for management prior to return
- ☐ Present summary with "deliverables"
- ☐ Set personal goals for yourself
- ☐ Institute positive change
- ☐ Keep in touch with new colleagues
- ☐ Send notes to speakers you enjoyed; get on their e-mail lists
- ☐ Thank supervisor for sending you

APPENDIX D

EXPENSES

Name:_____ Date:_____
Purpose of Trip/ Event:_____ Cost Center:_____

Day	Sunday	Monday	Tuesday	Wednesday	Thursday	Friday	Saturday	Total
Date								
Place of Departure								
Place of Arrival								
Mileage								
x mileage rate								
Tolls								
Parking								
Taxi								
Airfare								
Car Rental								
Hotel								
Breakfast								
Luncheon								
Dinner								
Entertainment								
Laundry								
Conference								
Books/Publications								
Gratuities								
Other Expenses								
Total								
Cash Advanced								
Balance Due								

Signature_____

Supervisor's Approval_____

Accounting_____

For reimbursement please give employee's name and address:

_____
_____
_____

NOTES

NOTES

NOTES

NOTES

NOTES

NOTES

NOTES